D0099668

peebles
PROSTHETICS INC.

Sofia
Soltani

PLEASANT HILL

13 Colonies

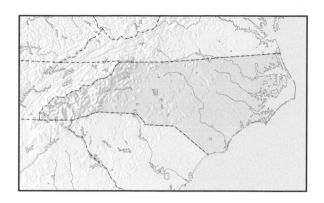

North Carolina

13 Colonies

NORTH CAROLINA

THE HISTORY OF NORTH CAROLINA COLONY, 1655–1776

ROBERTA WIENER AND JAMES R. ARNOLD

CONTRA COSTA COUNTY LIBRARY

3 1901 04310 2930

Raintree

Chicago, Illinois

© 2005 Raintree
Published by Raintree,
A division of Reed Elsevier, Inc.
Chicago, IL

All rights reserved. No part of this publication may be reproduced or transmitted in any form or by any means, electronic or mechanical, including photography, recording, taping, or any information storage and retrieval system, without permission in writing from the publishers.

For information, address the publisher:
Raintree, 100 N. LaSalle, Suite 1200, Chicago, IL 60602

Printed in China by South China Printing.
09 08 07 06 05
10 9 8 7 6 5 4 3 2 1

Library of Congress Cataloging-in-Publication Data
Wiener, Roberta, 1952-
  North Carolina / Roberta Wiener and James R. Arnold.
     p. cm. -- (13 colonies)
Summary: Examines the early colonization of North Carolina, discussing the struggles the colonists went through, their government, and daily lives. Includes bibliographical references and index.
  ISBN 0-7398-6885-3 (lib. bdg.) -- ISBN 1-4109-0309-5 (pbk.)
  1. North Carolina--History--Colonial period, ca. 1600-1775--Juvenile literature. [1. North Carolina--History--Colonial period, ca. 1600-1775.] I. Arnold, James R. II. Title. III. Series: Wiener, Roberta, 1952- 13 colonies.
  F257.W54 2004
  975.6'01--dc22
                        2003018473

Disclaimer
All the Internet addresses (URLs) given in this book were valid at the time of going to press. However, due to the dynamic nature of the Internet, some addresses may have changed, or sites may have changed or ceased to exist since publication. While the author and publishers regret any inconvenience this may cause readers, no responsibility for any such changes can be accepted by either the author or the publishers.

The paper used to print this book comes from sustainable resources.

Some words are shown in bold, **like this.** You can find out what they mean by looking in the glossary.

Previous page: Tryon Palace, a mansion built for the governor with 15,000 pounds of taxpayers' money, especially angered the poor back-country colonists and led to the formation of the Regulators.

Opposite; Fourth Creek, North Carolina, site of Fort Dobbs.

The authors wish to thank Walter Kossmann, whose knowledge, patience, and ability to ask all the right questions have made this a better series.

PICTURE ACKNOWLEDGMENTS

ARCHITECT OF THE CAPITOL: 8-9 AUTHORS: 17 WILLIAM CULLEN BRYANT, ET. AL., *Scribner's Popular History of the United States*, 1896: 16, 33 MARK CATESBY, *The Natural History of Carolina, Florida, and the Bahama Islands*, 1771: 34 top COLONIAL WILLIAMSBURG FOUNDATION: 6, 12, 23, 24, 26, 30-31, 36, 43 top, 44, 49 GUILFORD COURTHOUSE NATIONAL MILITARY PARK: 57 LIBRARY OF CONGRESS: 10, 14, 19, 42, 45, 53 BENSON J. LOSSING, *Our Country: A Household History of the United States*, 1895: 51 MOORE'S CREEK NATIONAL BATTLEFIELD: 56 NATIONAL ARCHIVES: Cover, 21, 43 bottom, 58 NATIONAL PARK SERVICE, COLONIAL NATIONAL HISTORICAL PARK: 24-25, 28-29, 38 COURTESY OF THE NORTH CAROLINA OFFICE OF ARCHIVES AND HISTORY: Title page, 5, 7, 11, 13, 15, 22, 27, 28, 32, 34 bottom, 37, 39, 40, 41, 46, 47, 48, 50, 52, 55, 59 SOUTH CAROLINA HISTORICAL SOCIETY: 35

Contents

PROLOGUE: THE WORLD IN 1584

By 1584, the year English people first came to Roanoke Island, North Carolina, Europeans had been exploring the wider world for more than 100 years. Advances in navigation and the building of better sailing ships made longer voyages possible. Great navigators from Portugal, Spain, Italy, the Netherlands, France, and England sailed into uncharted waters. The explorers reached Africa, India, the Pacific Ocean, China, and Japan. They encountered kingdoms and civilizations that had existed for centuries.

Europeans did not yet have a clear idea where all these lands lay, but they knew enough to see great opportunity. They saw the chance to grow rich from trade in exotic spices. They saw souls they wanted to convert to Christianity. They saw the chance to make conquests and expand their countries into great empires. And not least,

The world according to a European mapmaker around 1570

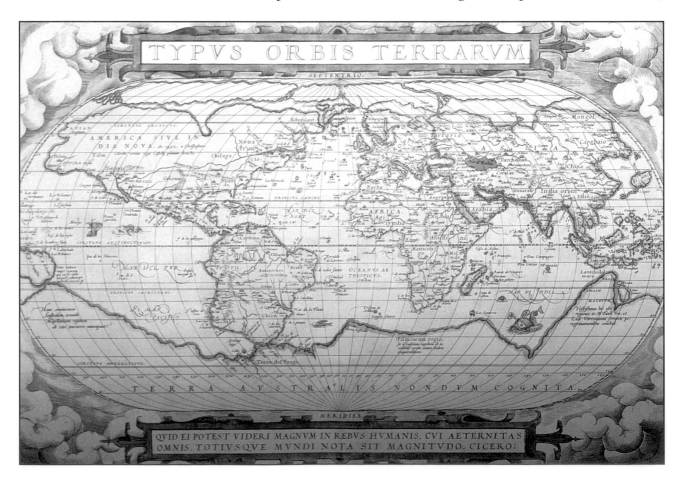

they encountered the dark-skinned people of Africa and, thinking them a different species, saw the chance to capture and sell them as slaves.

All the voyagers from Europe to the lands of the Pacific Ocean had to sail around Africa, a long and dangerous journey. So European explorers began to sail westward in search of shortcuts. In 1492, the explorer Christopher Columbus landed on an island on the far side of the Atlantic Ocean and claimed it for Spain. He thought that he had actually sailed all the way around the world and come to an island near India. Years of exploration by numerous sailors passed before the people of Europe realized that Columbus had been the first European of their era to set foot in a land unknown to them. They called this land the New World, although it was not new to the people who lived there.

A series of explorers landed on the eastern coast of

Alone among strangers in a new land, Europeans built forts for protection as soon as they arrived.

North America. The Italian seaman, Giovanni da Verrazano, commanded a French expedition in 1524 and explored and charted the North American coast from North Carolina to Maine. Of his first sighting of the North Carolina coast, Verrazano reported, "There appeared a new land which had never been seen before ... we realized that it was inhabited, for huge fires had been built on the seashore." Sailing the waters off present-day Hatteras Island, he spotted the waters of Pamlico Sound across the narrow island and believed he was seeing the Pacific Ocean.

A few years later, about 500 Spanish men and women, led by Lucas Vasquez de Ayllon, set out from a Caribbean island and settled near the Cape Fear River. Many died of malaria or hunger, and about 150 survivors plodded overland to Florida and to eventual rescue. The Spanish explorer Hernando de Soto led a party of soldiers overland from Florida to the Mississippi Valley, crossing the mountains in the southwestern corner of North Carolina in 1540. He was searching for gold.

By the time the English came to Roanoke, Jacques Cartier had claimed land for a French colony in present-day Canada. Far to the south, French **Protestants** had tried to start a colony in Florida and been ousted by the Spanish. The Spanish were far ahead of the French in the competition for land in the Americas. Before either the English or the French had settled in America, the Spanish had already claimed huge portions of both North and South America for Spain. They had conquered two mighty Native American empires, brought the first domestic horses to the Americas, and established a printing press and a university. In 1565 the Spanish founded the first permanent city, St. Augustine, in what would become the United States.

Yet there remained many places in this land where no Europeans had yet settled. Europeans saw America not just as a possible shortcut to somewhere else but as a huge empty land with riches waiting to be taken. The fact that a native people, the American **Indians**, had lived in America for perhaps 30,000 years did not figure in their calculations.

Hernando De Soto of Spain was the first European to reach the Mississippi River, after months of fighting Native Americans on his way through Alabama and Mississippi.

I.
A COLONY LOST

England lagged well behind Spain in the contest for the riches of America. In addition, England and Spain were enemies. Beginning in 1577, the English Admiral Sir Francis Drake had sailed around the world, explored parts of America, and attacked Spanish ships and settlements. In the meantime, Englishman Sir Humphrey Gilbert had made two voyages in the effort to set up a trading post in North America. He was lost at sea in 1583, and his patent, or royal permission, to explore and trade in America passed to his half brother, Walter Raleigh.

In the spring and summer of 1584, two English ships went on a voyage sponsored by Walter Raleigh. Commanded by Arthur Barlowe and Philip Amadas, the ships explored a small part of the coast of North America, the part that became present-day North Carolina. It was a beautiful time of year, with warm weather and plenty of food. The expedition returned to England with tempting descriptions of friendly natives, good hunting and fishing, and plentiful crops of corn and vegetables. Watercolors of the new land, painted by John White, created extra interest. The returning ships also carried two Native American men named Manteo and Wanchese. They were treated like celebrities in England. They learned to speak English and taught their language to some of their hosts.

Raleigh called the new land Virginia, in honor of Queen Elizabeth I, who was known as the Virgin Queen because she never married. In turn, she made Walter Raleigh a knight, and from then on he was known as Sir Walter Raleigh.

The following year, Raleigh sent a new expedition to the land called Virginia. One of his relatives, Sir Richard Grenville, commanded seven vessels that sailed from England in April 1585. The ships carried several hundred soldiers, a scientist, the artist John White, and the two **Native Americans**, Manteo and Wanchese. Raleigh planned for the group to establish a military outpost from which Spanish ships could be attacked.

Sir Francis Drake participated in important historical events on both sides of the Atlantic Ocean. He also played a small part in the history of Roanoke Island.

While exploring the North Carolina coast, the Englishmen met Native Americans, and John White painted pictures of their villages. One of the Native Americans helped himself to a silver cup belonging to the English. The Native Americans had a different view of property and freely gave and took possessions among themselves. However, in the English view this was theft. The English punished the Native Americans by burning a village and cornfields, taking the first step on the road to hostility.

The English ships reached Roanoke Island in late July, and Manteo and Wanchese returned to their people after an absence of nearly a year. The ships returned to England

The artist John White journeyed to Roanoke Island four times between 1584 and 1590. His watercolor of Native americans fishing is shown.

NATIVE AMERICANS: PEOPLE WHO HAD BEEN LIVING IN AMERICA FOR THOUSANDS OF YEARS AT THE TIME THE FIRST EUROPEANS ARRIVED

Queen Elizabeth I showered favors on Sir Walter Raleigh, and many people envied him.

leaving a garrison of 108 men, commanded by Ralph Lane, on Roanoke. The men built huts and defenses they called Fort Raleigh. They had arrived too late to plant many crops, and the island's soil was sandy and not very fertile. Also, some of their food supplies brought from England had been destroyed when one of their ships had run aground. When the expected supply ship from England failed to arrive, the men faced the prospect of a long hungry winter. They turned to the Native Americans for help.

The Native Americans did not have enough extra food to feed 108 unexpected guests through an entire winter.

John White's map of the coast shows the location of the Native American villages nearest to the English settlement.

Growing impatient with the Native Americans, Ralph Lane led his men in an attack on a Native American village and killed their chief. The Native Americans fled, leaving the English to fend for themselves. Lane's men somehow survived through the winter. They planted a spring crop of corn and waited for supply ships to arrive.

Meanwhile, Sir Francis Drake had been raiding Spanish settlements in the **West Indies** and Florida. On his way back to England, he stopped to visit the Roanoke settlement. Lane and his men decided to return to England. They left with Drake in June 1586, and Manteo went with them. However, they had made enemies among the Native Americans, and future settlers paid the price. Within a few days of their departure, Grenville, who had

WEST INDIES: THE ISLANDS OF THE CARIBBEAN SEA, SO CALLED BECAUSE THE FIRST EUROPEAN VISITORS THOUGHT THEY WERE CLOSE TO INDIA

led an earlier expedition and had sailed back to England, returned with food supplies and several hundred more men. After learning that the outpost had been abandoned, he left 15 men on the island, and put back out to sea.

Raleigh then sent a third expedition to colonize Virginia in May 1587. It consisted of 117 people, including 17 women and 9 children. John White was appointed governor. Manteo again made the return voyage to his homeland. This time, however, the English intended to settle on Chesapeake Bay, which a previous expedition had explored. They first stopped at Roanoke Island to return Manteo to his people and pick up the 15 men left behind the previous year. Shockingly, Simon Fernandez, the pilot

Left: John White's drawings have survived for hundreds of years, giving people today a good idea of what some Native Americans looked like when the first Europeans arrived. Captain Arthur Barlowe wrote of this chief, "The King is greatly obeyed, and his brothers and children reverenced."

Opposite: An artist's image of the baptism of Virginia Dare, the first English child born on Roanoke. Nine children sailed to Roanoke and at least two were born there.

of the ship that had brought them, refused to go farther and ordered the colonists set ashore at Roanoke.

On Roanoke the new colonists found one human skeleton, but no other trace of the fifteen men who had been left behind a year earlier. Within days, one of the new colonists was killed by Native Americans while he was out gathering crabs. Again the settlers had arrived too late to grow crops. Having been unexpectedly marooned on inhospitable Roanoke, the colonists planned to move. Some were to cross to the mainland, and some to Croatoan, the island on which Manteo's people lived. They feared that supply ships would be unable to find them. So shortly after the birth of his granddaughter, Virginia Dare—the first English child born in America— John White re-embarked to sail to England to report his colonists' location and their desperate need for supplies.

When White returned to England, the country was on the brink of war with Spain, and few people besides Raleigh set much importance on the plight of the colonists. In April 1588, Raleigh and White managed to outfit two ships with supplies for a return to Roanoke. On the crossing, the two captains they had hired started raiding enemy ships. But instead of capturing ships, their ships were taken, along with all of White's supplies. White returned again to England barely a month after he had left.

White and Raleigh worked hard to gather more supplies and ships, but all seemed to conspire against them. After a three year absence, White returned to Roanoke Island in August 1590. The island was deserted, the houses gone. As agreed, the departing colonists had left a message, the word "CROATOAN" carved on a post. White assumed that the colonists had moved to Croatoan, present-day Ocracoke Island and the home of their friend Manteo. A fierce storm, probably a hurricane, forced White's ships out to sea before they could sail to Croatoan, and instead they returned to England once again.

John White was never again able to search for his lost colony, his lost daughter and grandchild. Three years after his last voyage, he wrote sadly that he was forced to leave the fate of his colonists "to the merciful help of the Almighty, whom I most humbly be-seech to help & comfort them...." With those words, John White disappeared from history.

The remains of the Lost Colony. Many historians have assumed that Simon Fernandez left the colonists on Roanoke Island because he was in a hurry to put out to sea. However, the historian Lee Miller suggests that Fernandez may have been in the pay of an enemy of Walter Raleigh, and that this enemy wanted Raleigh's colony to fail. Raleigh's rights to the land were due to expire if he failed to plant a successful colony by 1590. Roanoke was already known to be a risky place for a settlement, and Fernandez may have intended all along to leave the colonists there to perish.

2.
NORTH CAROLINA IN 1590

North Carolina was once covered with trees, from the scrubby pines and oaks of the coastal plain to the towering forests of the Appalachian Mountains. The seacoast is guarded by a chain of barrier islands, whose shifting sands and currents have destroyed as many as 5,000 ships. Heading inland, the coastal plain, or Tidewater region, covers nearly half of North Carolina's land area. Next lies the piedmont region, then the Appalachian Mountains, including the Blue Ridge and Great Smoky Mountains. Mount Mitchell, at 6,684 feet, (2,037 meters) is the highest peak in the eastern United States. The climate varies as widely as the landscape, from subtropical conditions in the southeastern coastal area to a cooler mountain climate with harsh winters in the northwest. Palmetto trees and Venus flytraps are native plants of North Carolina's subtropical zone. Deer, rabbits, squirrels, possum, and raccoons live throughout the state, and bear and wildcats live in the mountains.

The Carolinas have been inhabited by people for about 10,000 years. More than 30,000 Native Americans lived in the area at the time the first Europeans arrived. They were divided into numerous tribes belonging to one of three linguistic groups. The Algonquian-speaking tribes lived along the coast, the Siouan peoples lived in the hilly country of the Piedmont, and a powerful tribe known as the Cherokee, who spoke an Iroquoian language, lived in

View of the Atlantic Ocean from the Outer Banks

EPIDEMIC: WIDESPREAD OUTBREAK OF CONTAGIOUS DISEASE; FOR EXAMPLE, IN 1738, A SMALLPOX EPIDEMIC KILLED HALF OF ALL CHEROKEES.

Forests still cover the mountains in western North Carolina.

the west along the Blue Ridge Mountains. Before the first Europeans arrived, North Carolina was a battleground between the Iroquoian and Siouan tribes.

North Carolina's coastal Native Americans welcomed the English and were eager to trade with them. However, Roanoke Island's first English settlers, the soldiers of Fort Raleigh in 1585, attacked the coastal Native Americans, turning them against the English. However, by the time English people again tried to settle in North Carolina, in the 1660s, the passage of time had worked in their favor. The memory of the English attacks had faded, and the Native American population had been reduced by **epidemic** diseases caught from the earliest English colonists.

About 1,000 Native Americans lived along the Cape Fear River near the southeastern coast of North Carolina. They came to be called the Cape Fear Indians. English settlers came to the area in the early 1660s. They, too, mistreated the Native Americans, seizing some of their children and selling them into slavery, while pretending that they were sending the children away to learn the ways of European civilization. In spite of such treatment, the Cape Fear Indians cooperated with the settlers.

Engravings based on John White's drawings of Native Americans. A walled village appears in the background of the lower picture.

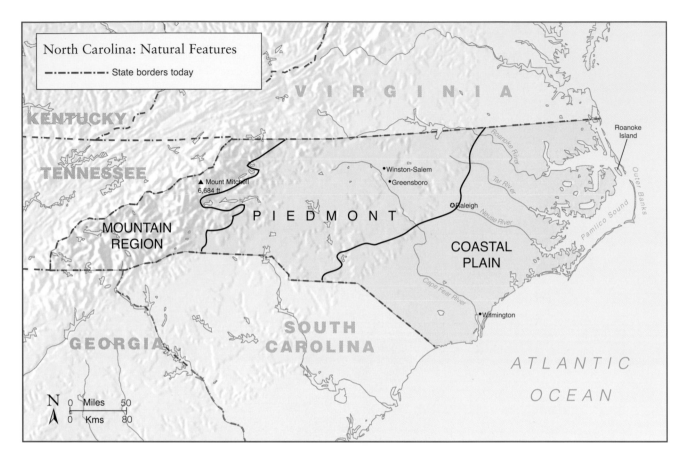

North Carolina: Natural Features

------- State borders today

VIRGINIA

KENTUCKY

TENNESSEE

▲ Mount Mitchell
6,684 ft

MOUNTAIN
REGION

PIEDMONT

•Winston-Salem
•Greensboro

Roanoke River

Tar River

⊕Raleigh

Neuse River

Roanoke
Island

Outer Banks

Pamlico Sound

COASTAL
PLAIN

GEORGIA

SOUTH
CAROLINA

Cape Fear River

•Wilmington

ATLANTIC

OCEAN

N

0   Miles   50

0   Kms   80

At the time of the first known contact with English colonists, the Chowanoc were the dominant tribe in northeastern North Carolina. They belonged to the Algonquian linguistic family and were allied with other Algonquian tribes in North Carolina. Their population numbered about 1,500.

The Tuscarora were a confederacy of three Iroquois tribes who lived along major rivers in the Piedmont region. This confederacy numbered about 5,000 people. Among the tribes that lived to the west of the Tuscarora were the Cheraw. About 1,200 Cheraw lived along the South Carolina border from the Piedmont to the mountains. The Cheraw probably belonged to the Siouan linguistic family.

The Cherokee were the best known of the tribes living in the western mountains of North Carolina. The Cherokee established trading relations with English traders soon after the first English colonists arrived.

These Native Americans lived in villages surrounded by protective fences. They built their houses of bark and woven

Cypress trees on the Neuse River, along which the Tuscarora lived .

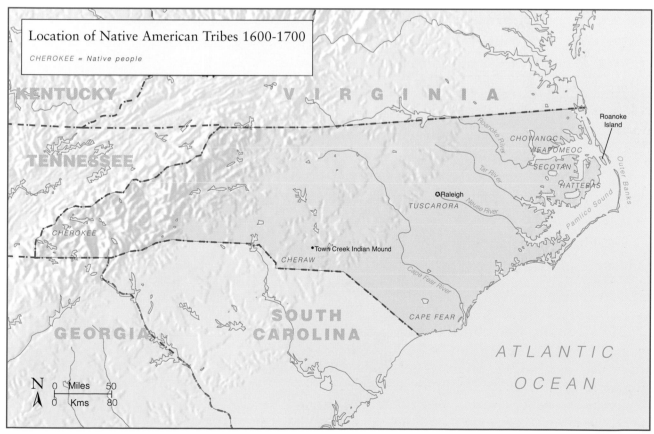

Location of Native American Tribes 1600-1700

CHEROKEE = Native people

KENTUCKY

VIRGINIA

TENNESSEE

Roanoke Island

CHOWANOC

WEAPOMEOC

Roanoke River

Tar River

SECOTAN

HATTERAS

Outer Banks

⊕Raleigh

TUSCARORA

Neuse River

Pamlico Sound

CHEROKEE

•Town Creek Indian Mound

CHERAW

Cape Fear River

SOUTH CAROLINA

CAPE FEAR

GEORGIA

ATLANTIC OCEAN

N

0 Miles 50
0 Kms 80

mats placed over a framework of poles. Near their homes they prepared large fields for farming. They made small mounds within these fields where they planted corn along with squash and beans. They also grew tobacco, and eventually introduced the English to smoking. During the summer, women tended the fields, which the men had cleared. They usually managed to grow or find just enough food to survive.

The Native Americans also lived by hunting and fishing. The Carolinas were rich in wildlife. The ocean and rivers yielded tremendous amounts of fish and shellfish. Huge populations of waterfowl such as ducks and geese lived in the coastal marshes. The inland forests gave food and shelter to an abundance of wild animals. Deer and deerskins provided the people with food, clothing, and shelter.

John White's drawing of the Native American village of Secota opens a window on a way of life that existed more than 400 years ago.

3.
THE RETURN OF THE ENGLISH

Many months went by before people in England realized that Raleigh's colony at Roanoke had met with a mysterious end. Meanwhile, returning explorers—along with several Native Americans they brought back to England—continued to tell about the wonders and riches of America and encouraged people to settle there. They brought back ships full of furs and told of abundant fish and thick forests full of valuable, tall trees. However, the barrier islands made it dangerous to approach the colony from the sea. They had prevented John White from returning to find his lost colony, and they prevented other Europeans from establishing settlements. Not until English settlers traveled overland from Jamestown, would the English succeed in colonizing the land that would come to be called Carolina.

Queen Elizabeth died in 1603, and James I, her distant cousin, became king of England. King James, under the influence of Raleigh's enemies, accused Raleigh of treason, imprisoned him for life, and stripped him of his rights to Virginia. Other English people took over the drive to gain the rewards of America.

A group of these men, led by one of Raleigh's rivals, asked the king for permission to colonize the rich land known as Virginia. The king granted them a **charter** in 1606, permitting them to form a trading company and settle there. The new company, called the Virginia Company of London, included

Sir Walter Raleigh supported colonization efforts, but never visited North America.

"certain Knights, gentlemen, merchants, and adventurers, of our city of London and elsewhere." These men wanted mainly to make money for themselves and the company's shareholders. The first English settlers of Virginia were trying to find gold and other valuable products to sell in England, and to search for a waterway that would serve as a shortcut to the Pacific Ocean.

The colonists of Jamestown, Virginia, arrived in 1607, beginning the first surviving English settlement. The English had not forgotten Roanoke. Soon after they arrived, the Jamestown colonists sent a search party to look for survivors from Roanoke Island. The searchers spoke with various Native Americans and heard that some of the lost colonists may have lived with friendly Native Americans for a time, but that an enemy tribe had killed them. Some evidence exists of Native Americans with gray eyes who may have descended from English people of the lost colony. The searchers also heard that seven English people still survived and were forced by a chieftain to be slaves in a remote copper mine. The Native Americans assured the searchers that the keeper of these slaves would never give them up. Failing to contact any survivors, the Jamestown colonists called off the search. It was easier to assume that the lost colonists were dead, easier to stop searching for survivors, and easier still to blame the Native Americans for the lost colonists' fate.

Failing to find the lost English people, the Jamestown colonists remained interested in the possible sources of wealth that existed in the land to the south. Over the

Above: King Charles I the son of King James I, ruled England from 1625 to 1649.

Right: The Jamestown colony suffered an astounding death rate in its early years, but it eventually prospered.

King Charles II, son of Charles I,
ruled England from 1660 to 1685.

next 20 years, they wrote to England about the land's resources in glowing terms.

In 1629, King Charles I granted a charter to one of his officials, Sir Robert Heath. The king gave the name "Carolana" to an area extending from Spanish Florida to Virginia. Heath made plans to colonize the land but had no success. One expedition sailed from England, but the captain delivered the would-be colonists to Jamestown. Heath gave up his charter and other men tried to start a new colony, publishing pamphlets in an effort to stimulate interest among the English.

The first English people to live in the land of Carolana were men from Jamestown. In fact, they saw Carolana as simply the southern part of Virginia. By the 1650s, Virginians were going south to buy land from the Native

PROPRIETOR: PRIVATE OWNER

Americans, and the Virginia government was making land grants in the region. In 1655, a fur trader named Nathaniel Batts became probably the first English person to live in the area that became modern-day North Carolina. He lived in a small house on land purchased from the Native Americans about forty miles south of Jamestown. As Virginia's population grew and land became scarce, more traders and farmers bought land from the Native Americans and expanded southward into the area around Albemarle Sound. In 1662, Virginia's governor appointed officials to govern what he called the "Southern Plantation."

England had been plunged into civil war since 1649, and King Charles I was executed. After years in exile, the son of Charles I was restored to the throne and became King Charles II in 1660. The new king rewarded eight of his most loyal supporters by granting them the vast area of Carolana, renaming it Carolina. The land grant extended not only from Florida to Virginia, but all the way to the Pacific Ocean. The **proprietors** divided the northern part of Carolina into two regions: Albemarle, the northeastern part of North Carolina bordering Virginia; and Clarendon, along the Cape Fear River toward present-day South Carolina. The charter of March 24, 1663, gave the new proprietors power to grant land, appoint public officials, collect taxes, and raise armies to conduct wars. They were

The Charter of 1663

Left: Sir George Carteret held an honorary post in England as chamberlain, or director, of the royal household.

Center: George Monck, Duke of Albemarle. The name Albemarle was given to one of the original counties, and Virginians referred to part of early North Carolina as Albemarle. Monck was captain-general of the king's armed forces.

Right: Lord William Craven, described in the charter as "right trusty and wellbeloved."

required, however, to consult an elected **assembly**. The first assembly met under a tree in Albemarle County in 1665. The charter also called for official tolerance of religions that differed from the Church of England. This provision arose from the desire to attract settlers and increase the English population, rather than from a firm belief in religious freedom.

One of the proprietors, Sir William Berkeley, was already the governor of Virginia. Two others, Lord John Berkeley, William's brother, and Sir George Carteret were also the proprietors of New Jersey colony. The other five proprietors were George Monck, the Duke of Albemarle; Edward Hyde, Earl of Clarendon; Lord William Craven; Anthony Ashley Cooper, Earl of Shaftesbury; and Sir John Colleton. Most of these proprietors were content to rule their colony from England.

The Virginia settlers who had arrived before Carolina was chartered lived a pioneer's life of **subsistence** farming and handmade goods. They cut down the trees to clear land, build log cabins, and fuel their cooking fires. The new proprietors, however, expected to make money by granting large tracts of land and collecting rents. They were not looking for **pioneers** who wanted to make a bare living on small farms. The proprietors tried to recruit settlers from New England and from the island of Barbados. Colonists came from each, but many did not like Carolina and returned home.

In 1669, the proprietors put into effect the "Fundamental Constitutions of Carolina." This impractical document called for a **feudal** society based on members of the **nobility** owning large tracts of land that would be worked by tenant farmers. However, it

Colonial wine-making. Several of the proprietors sponsored the man they had appointed deputy governor, Peter Carteret, in a large plantation dedicated to making a profit by growing grapes to make wine, raising hogs and cattle, and whaling. Only the whale oil proved profitable.

continued the elected **legislature** and the policy of religious tolerance for non-**Anglican** Christians. The 1669 constitution gave Jews as well the right to openly practice their religion in Carolina. The proprietors may have been trying to attract the many prosperous Jewish traders who lived on Barbados in the West Indies, in order to expand Carolina's population of barely 4,000. The first Anglican minister did not arrive in the colony until 1701, and only then did the colony's government officially establish the Anglican church. Even so, many denominations, including the **Quakers**, continued to coexist in Carolina.

In 1670, about 200 colonists from Barbados founded Charles Town (Charleston in present day South Carolina), named after the king. The small island of Barbados had become extremely crowded, with more than 30,000 people on an island of 166 square miles. Many islanders were attracted by the generous offer of land. The proprietors granted colonists 150 acres per family member or slave, and set a rent of half a penny per

LEGISLATURE: GROUP OF REPRESENTATIVES ELECTED TO MAKE LAWS

ANGLICAN: BELONGING TO THE CHURCH OF ENGLAND, A PROTESTANT CHURCH AND THE STATE church of England

QUAKER: ORIGINALLY A TERM OF MOCKERY GIVEN TO MEMBERS OF THE SOCIETY OF FRIENDS, A CHRISTIAN GROUP FOUNDED IN ENGLAND AROUND 1650

NAVIGATION: SCIENCE OF
FIGURING OUT ONE'S
POSITION AND DIRECTION
WHEN TRAVELING ON THE
OCEAN

MILITIA: GROUP OF
CITIZENS NOT NORMALLY
PART OF THE ARMY WHO
JOIN TOGETHER TO
DEFEND THEIR LAND IN AN
EMERGENCY

Charles Town was renamed
Charleston soon after the
American Revolution.

acre, with no payment due until 1689. **Planters** wealthy enough to own numerous slaves received unimaginably huge tracts of land.

The proprietors supported the **navigation** acts passed by England in 1673. These laws limited the colonies to trading only with England. Also, if colonists sent trade goods to the other colonies, the law required them to pay a tax. When, in 1677, the proprietors directed a new deputy governor, Thomas Miller, to enforce the laws and collect taxes, a group that opposed the laws tried to prevent Miller from taking office. Miller succeeded in taking office with the help of the **militia**, but his efforts to collect taxes led to an armed rebellion. Two prominent planters, George Durant and John Culpeper, led an armed revolt that put Miller in jail. The revolt became known as Culpeper's Rebellion. Miller was brought to trial by the rebels, but escaped and fled to England.

The proprietors then appointed as governor the newest proprietor, Seth Sothel, who had bought Edward Hyde's

Above: A coin called the "Elephant Token" was issued by the proprietors in 1694.

Above: Governor Edward Hyde, a descendant of the proprietor of the same name, asked the neighboring colonies for help fighting the Tuscaroras in 1711. He died the following year in an epidemic of yellow fever.

share of Carolina. On the way from England to Carolina, Sothel was captured by pirates and spent five years in prison in northern Africa. He finally escaped and arrived to govern the colony in 1683. Sothel proved to be such a corrupt governor that the assembly arrested him and expelled him from Carolina in 1689.

Eventually, the colony settled down under an acceptable government. The governor of Carolina ruled from present-day Charleston, South Carolina. A deputy governor ruled the Albemarle region, the name given to part of present-day North Carolina. In 1712, the vast Carolina territory was divided and North Carolina and South Carolina officially became two separate colonies. The proprietors realized that the territory was too large to be governed effectively from a single capital at Charles Town.

The government of North Carolina consisted of a two-house legislature: an upper house with the governor and his appointed council, and an elected assembly. Only **freemen**—white men over the age of 21, who had lived in the colony for at least a year and had paid their taxes—had the right to vote. North Carolina's legislature held its meetings in homes or taverns around the settlement that later became Edenton. Public records were kept at someone's house, and the governor's seal was hidden in a barrel. Copies of new laws were written out by hand, since the colony had no printing press. The only public building was a log structure that served as the prison. Not until 1718 was a courthouse built, and in 1722 the capital was officially established at the town of Edenton, where it remained for about twenty years.

THE TUSCARORA WAR

Many of the Native Americans of North Carolina at first welcomed the English colonists and hoped the English would protect them from rival tribes. The Chowanoc made a treaty with the English in 1663. In 1695, the Cape Fear Indians asked to be taken under the protection of the English and helped the English in campaigns against rival tribes. The Tuscarora coexisted peacefully with the colonists and came to rely on trading with them. However, in time the Tuscarora grew to distrust the English traders. The traders charged high prices—reckoned in deer skins—

Carolina planters encouraged Indians to capture rival Indians and sell them as slaves. In return the Indians received guns and ammunition. They did not know how to make their own firearms, so they became dependent on the colonists for them. Since Indian slaves kept on Carolina plantations could escape by slipping away into the woods, most captive Indians were shipped to the West Indies.

FREEMEN: WHITE, TAXPAYING MALES OF AT LEAST 21 YEARS OF AGE WHO POSSESSED ALL THE RIGHTS OF CITIZENSHIP, SUCH AS THE RIGHT TO VOTE, HOLD PUBLIC OFFICE, OR OWN LAND

for English goods such as guns and ammunition, cloth, pots, and tools. The traders also kidnapped Native American women and children and sold them into slavery.

The breaking point came in 1710, when Baron Christoph von Graffenreid purchased a huge tract of land in Carolina and led a group of about 400 Swiss, German, and English settlers to build the town of New Bern. This new and substantial settlement, in addition to the traders cheating and enslaving of their people, convinced the Tuscarora that it was time to drive the white people from Carolina.

At dawn on September 22, 1711, in a well-planned, surprise attack, about 500 Tuscarora and their Native American allies moved from farm to farm, killing about 130 colonists who lived around New Bern. They hideously butchered some of their victims, and took about two dozen women and children captive. The disorganized colonists made a few unsuccessful attempts to take revenge. One group of enraged colonists captured a Native American and burned him alive. The Native Americans attacked with renewed ferocity, burning farms, destroying crops, and stealing cattle. The colonists retreated and gathered at several outlying farms and plantations, which they tried to fortify. The deputy

John Lawson and the Indians of Carolina

John Lawson arrived in Carolina in 1701. The proprietors hired him to study and report on their province. He started out from Charles Town and traveled throughout both Carolinas, visiting many Indian villages along the way. In his book about his travels, *A New Voyage to Carolina*, published in 1709, he wrote of the Indians: "They are really better to us, than we are to them; they always give us [food] at their quarters … we do not do so by them … but let them walk by our doors hungry."

Lawson bought land in eastern North Carolina and stayed in the colony for the rest of his life. A friend and admirer of the Indians, he died at their hands. In September 1711, Lawson, along with Christoph von Graffenreid and two slaves, went exploring up the Neuse River. They were captured by the Tuscarora, who executed Lawson, thinking he was trying to claim their land, but spared the others. They may have believed Graffenreid was the colonial governor, and they generally sympathized with black slaves. The Indians revealed to von Graffenreid their plan to attack the colonists, but he remained a prisoner and could not warn the population. The Tuscarora War followed.

Mark Catesby arrived in the Carolinas in 1722 to study and paint the wildlife. The Carolina Parakeet (above) is now extinct. John Lawson, too, observed the parakeet and described it in his book: "They are often taken alive, and will become familiar and tame in two days ….They devour the birch buds in April, and lie hidden when the weather is frosty and hard." Unlike Lawson, Catesby understood that the birds did not "lie hidden" in winter, but instead, "retire more south."

Left: The Tuscarora capture John Lawson and his companions.

governor pleaded with the neighboring colonies for help. The governor at Charles Town responded by sending Colonel John Barnwell in command of about 500 Yamassee warriors who were longtime enemies of the Tuscarora.

Months of fierce fighting finally convinced the Tuscarora to surrender and return their captives. They signed a peace treaty in April 1712. As Barnwell and his troops headed back home, some of his men defied orders and captured Native Americans to be sold as slaves. The Tuscarora were angered by this conduct and resumed their raids against the terrorized colonists. Again the North Carolina government appealed to their southern neighbors for help. In November 1712, Charles Town sent Colonel James Moore, a few dozen militia officers, and 1,000 Native American warriors to fight the Tuscarora.

Moore's force killed or captured nearly 1,000 Tuscarora men, women, and children. Many were sold into slavery. This massive defeat ended large-scale Native American attacks on North Carolina settlers, and a new treaty was signed in the spring of 1713. A few Tuscarora made isolated raids, but Moore's men hunted them down. In 1715, the Tuscarora signed another treaty agreeing to cease all raids and to move to a reservation. Instead, most of the Tuscarora moved north to New York colony, to join the Iroquois of the Five Nations.

Just two months later, North Carolina had the chance to repay South Carolinians for their help. The Yamassee Indians, who had helped fight the Tuscarora, joined with other Native Americans to kill South Carolina traders whom they believed had cheated them. North Carolina sent two militia companies to help defeat the Yamassee.

Colonel Barnwell and his fighting men march to the aid of North Carolina.

4.
THE GROWING COLONY

The end of the Tuscarora and Yamassee wars opened the way for more colonists to settle in the Carolinas. Native Americans withdrew to the west or were confined to reservations, their numbers reduced by war and disease. Where once more than ten thousand Native Americans had lived, only a few hundred remained. The tide of white settlement swept across the colony, bringing small subsistence farms, large plantations, and colonial towns.

Still, the population remained small in comparison to that of other colonies. The black population grew faster than the white population because plantations used numerous slaves to do all the work. From about 9,000 whites and only a few hundred blacks in 1700, by 1730 the white population had tripled to about 27,000 while the black population increased more than tenfold to over 5,000. By the Revolution, one person in three was black and a slave.

North Carolina plantations grew tobacco, rice, or indigo (the source of a blue dye) for export. Many smaller farms produced enough surplus corn, pork, and beef to export. The pine forests of the east provided the raw materials for the production of naval stores: tar,

Sir Francis Drake brought the first tobacco from the Americas to England, where it became instantly and hugely popular. Small planters in the northern half of North Carolina grew tobacco. Despite the popularity of smoking in Europe, an oversupply of tobacco caused prices to fall. Taxes and low prices left colonial planters with little profit.

pitch, rosin, and turpentine for ship building and maintenance. Other forest products included timbers for ship masts, lumber, wood shingles, and barrels. The colony also exported furs and deer hides, and imported most manufactured items as well as clothing and household goods.

Four North Carolina communities had ship landings that served as ports: Roanoke, Bath, Beaufort, and Brunswick, near Wilmington. The channels leading to these landings were too shallow to permit entry of large trading ships. The larger ships used the seaports at Charles Town and the Chesapeake Bay. The Outer Banks, the barrier islands along North Carolina's coast, came to be called the "Graveyard of the Atlantic," because so many shipwrecks occurred there. Ships attempting to reach the shallow ports of North Carolina also ran the risk of being taken by pirates.

Pirates found the North Carolina coast an especially good place from which to launch their attacks on trading

Carolina planters began growing rice after 1685, when a ship captain brought some seeds from Madagascar. Slaves planted rice in April or May. Fields were flooded in the summer. Following harvest in September or October, slaves spent long hours shaking the rice grains from the stalks and pounding the grains of rice to remove the husks.

Famous Pirates

The pirate Edward Teach was known as Blackbeard. He was born in an English seaport and went to sea on a trading ship. After serving as a seaman on a privateer he turned to piracy. It is reported that he married and was welcome in high society anywhere in North Carolina. Finally, in 1718, a party of Virginians set sail to capture him and his ship, the Adventure. They found the pirate's ship off Ocracoke Island. The Virginians killed Blackbeard and nine of his men, cutting off Blackbeard's head and hanging it on their ship for all to see. Blackbeard's other crewmen were captured and taken to Virginia, where they were tried and executed.

Stede Bonnet was a wealthy and educated man, a former British army major. He retired from the army and settled on Barbados where he had a fine house. Perhaps the urge for adventure caused him to join with Blackbeard. From Black-beard's band, he went out on his own, raiding South Carolina shipping from his base of operations on the Cape Fear River near the border between the two Carolinas. South Carolina's governor sent an expedition to put an end to Bonnet's piracy. Bonnet and 29 of his men were captured and taken to Charles Town, where they were executed in 1718.

Left: The Virginians advertised their successful mission by hanging Blackbeard's head from the yardarm of their ship.

Below: The execution of Major Stede Bonnet

pirates and turned a blind eye to their activities. The neighboring colonies of South Carolina and Virginia, each with a major seaport, were losing too many ships loaded with merchandise to the pirates of North Carolina. Each of these colonies, in the face of inaction by North Carolina officials, took matters into their own hands and set out to capture the most notorious pirates, Blackbeard and Major Stede Bonnet. In 1718, they succeeded, capturing and executing the ringleaders and more than 50 other pirates.

As the American colonies grew more populous and wealthy, the government of **Great Britain** began seeking more control over them. At the same time, some elements in the Carolinas despised the proprietors and petitioned the king to take over. The eight original proprietors of North and South Carolina had died and most of their descendants were not making enough money from the colonies to remain interested in ownership. In 1729, all but one of the heirs agreed to sell their colonial land back to the king, and both North and South Carolina became royal colonies. Only John Carteret, the heir of Sir George Carteret, held onto his share, and kept ownership of a huge piece of land equivalent to one eighth of the land area of the Carolinas. Although he still owned the land, which he held until the Revolution, he no longer had the right to govern it. This right had passed to the king and the royal governors he appointed.

North Carolina's first royal governors tried to collect rents for all the land occupied by settlers, but many refused to pay. The assembly also tried to limit the governors' power by refusing to pass laws. Gabriel Johnston, who became governor in 1734, at first reported that it was, "impossible to do business with them," but he was able to work out a deal with the assembly to make the government work again. He agreed to recognize old land claims by people who had not followed proper procedures, and in return the assembly agreed to his plan for rent collection. Still, rents remained difficult to collect for many years.

North Carolina shared a long boundary with Virginia, and the two colonies argued over its exact location. In 1728, the two colonies conducted a joint survey and set an official boundary. The two Carolinas then conducted a survey to set a dividing line in 1737, but arguments continued to break out over where the line should be.

GREAT BRITAIN: NATION FORMED BY ENGLAND, WALES, SCOTLAND, AND NORTHERN IRELAND; THE TERM "GREAT BRITAIN" CAME INTO USE WHEN ENGLAND AND SCOTLAND FORMALLY UNIFIED IN 1707.

The Virginia-North Carolina border crosses the Great Dismal Swamp (below). Roads across North Carolina's many wetland areas had to be corduroyed, or covered with logs, to prevent wagons from getting bogged down. Colonists were required to work several days each year on public roads.

Moravians under attack in Europe. The Moravian church began in the 1400s as a Christian religious movement in a part of eastern Europe called Moravia. A very small group of people kept the religion going in secret in spite of centuries of persecution. The first Moravians came to America during the 1730s. Moravian and Presbyterian ministers could legally perform marriages in the colony despite the fact that only the Anglican church was officially established.

From the 1730s until the Revolution, North Carolina's white population grew from about 30,000 to more than 150,000, fueled by waves of immigration from Europe and the other colonies. During the same period, the black slave population grew more than tenfold to more than 70,000. The mild climate, the availability of land, and the tolerance of different religions attracted Scottish Presbyterians, British Quakers, and German and Swiss Moravians. In 1732, a wave of immigration from Scotland began. Also during the 1730s, Pennsylvania settlers, including German and **Scotch-Irish** immigrants, began moving along the Great Wagon Road, which ran down the Shenandoah Valley of western Virginia. They settled on land in the North Carolina Piedmont region.

Many more Scotch-Irish people came to North Carolina after 1754, the year Arthur Dobbs, also Scotch-Irish, became governor of the colony. Whole communities of Scottish people continued for decades to speak their native language, Gaelic, in North Carolina. German immigrants also continued to use their native language for many years. Within 20 years, about 20% of North Carolina's people were Scottish and about 5% were German.

Moravians from Pennsylvania moved as a group to North Carolina. They obtained land in 1753 and built the community of Bethabara. In 1766 they began building Salem. Both towns became a part of modern-day Winston-Salem. Among its many accomplishments, the hard-working group built a system of wood pipes that brought water into each home.

5.
EAST AND WEST

Planters and wealthy townspeople in the eastern part of the colony considered themselves to be of a higher social class than the more modest farmers and tradesmen of both the eastern and western regions. However, even eastern North Carolina colonists lived far from major ports and were not as wealthy as the upper classes in Virginia and South Carolina, so they could not follow the latest fashions in clothing and furnishings. Many lived in large brick houses with proper glass windows, in contrast to the small wood frame cottages or log cabins of **frontier** dwellers. People who didn't farm or own plantations pursued such businesses and trades as operating ferries, keeping taverns, making furniture, and building ships. The wealthiest merchants and traders, attorneys, and public officials made up the town **elites**.

The wealthy plantation owners came to control much of the political power of the colonies. Many became lawyers and then went into politics. When mosquitos

Above: Wealthy people imported fashionable clothing from England.

Below: A North Carolina plantation house

"Dancing they are all fond of, especially when they can get a fiddle or bag-pipe; at this they will continue hours together," reported Dr. John Brickell of Edenton. Wealthy colonists enjoyed such entertainment as dancing, card playing, fox hunting, and horse racing. The less wealthy enjoyed hunting, fishing, and going to taverns to meet their friends.

infested their riverside plantations in the summer, they moved to their townhouses along the coast to join in the social whirl and political activities. While at home on their plantations, they spent long hours supervising their slaves.

The field slaves, in turn, did all the hard work of growing and harvesting plantation crops. House slaves catered to their owners' every need, cooking and serving meals, cleaning, and even helping people bathe and dress. Most slave owners saw nothing wrong with owning people to do all their work. A pamphlet published in Britain to recruit colonists boasted, "Young healthy negroes are bought there for between 25 and 40 **pounds**. Five of these will clear and labor a plantation for the first year, so as you shall have every thing in abundance for your family, with little trouble to yourself." Another planter saw things differently, writing that slaves "blow up the pride and ruin the industry of our white people, who seeing a rank of poor creatures below them, detest work for fear it should make them look like slaves."

By contrast, farmers who settled on North Carolina's western frontier lived as pioneers, clearing the trees off their land, building their own small cabins, and making their own furniture and clothing. Every member of the family, from an early age, had work to do caring for crops and livestock. Frontier children had little time for schoolwork.

North Carolina's few schools were run by churches. The first school to be supported by public money was established in 1766 in New Bern. Most colonial parents had to pay for their children's entire education. Children of wealthy families were taught by private tutors, and older sons went on to academies and colleges in Virginia,

Slave-owning colonists thought that Africans, coming from a hot land, were better able to endure hard work in the hot southern climate. In fact, many slaves died from being forced to work too hard in the intense heat.

the northern colonies, or Great Britain. Children from less wealthy families were taught to read and write by parents or relatives, or they attended country schools paid for by their parents. Orphans or the children of poor parents were often apprenticed to learn a trade until they were 21 years old. Masters were expected to make sure their apprentices learned to read.

Above: Fine mansions and modest cabins alike had wood shingles on their roofs.

Right: Farmers allowed cattle and hogs to run loose in the woods. The farm animals stayed out in the woods throughout the mild winters. Farmers kept track of ownership with branding or earmarks, and registered their marks and brands in county records. The brands are shown in the right-hand column.

The Boones: A Frontier Family

Daniel Boone was born on a 250-acre farm in Berks County in what is today eastern Pennsylvania. In 1734, the year of his birth, it was the western frontier of white settlement in Pennsylvania. Boone's grandfather was an English Quaker who had heard of William Penn's Quaker haven, and he moved his family there from Great Britain by 1717. Daniel Boone was the sixth child born to Squire and Sarah Boone. Two of the Boone children married non-Quakers. They and their father were expelled from the society. As a result, Squire Boone decided to leave Pennsylvania. In 1750, the family traveled down the Shenandoah Valley of Virginia, as did many other migrants to North Carolina. The Boones first tried farming in Virginia, but moved on to North Carolina in 1751. By 1753, the Boones had settled on a 640-acre farm on the far western frontier, in present-day Davidson County, south of Winston-Salem.

Young Daniel had little or no education but had learned, just barely, to read and write. From an early age, he could shoot very well and loved to hunt above all. Although he worked on his parents' farms in Pennsylvania and North Carolina, his greatest contribution was putting meat on the table. Soon after the family's move to North Carolina, Daniel Boone served as a wagoner, hauling supplies for General Braddock's ill-fated expedition in the opening days of the French and Indian War.

Boone married Rebecca Bryan in 1756. Over the course of their life together they had ten children. They continued to live and farm in North Carolina, but as the population grew, Daniel went on long hunting expeditions and looked for a new land to settle. His long hunts took him to Florida, the Virginia frontier, and finally, to Kentucky in the late 1760s. He blazed a trail through the Cumberland Gap into Kentucky, and this later came to be called the Wilderness Road. In 1773, Boone led his own and other North Carolina families to settle in Kentucky, but they were forced to turn back by attacking Cherokees. Two years later, the settlers tried again and succeeded in founding Boonesborough.

In the end, neither frontier North Carolina nor Kentucky were far enough from civilization for him. Along with his son, Daniel Boone went on to Missouri as a hunter and trapper in 1799. He died in 1820 at the age of 86, in St. Charles County, Missouri, which was by then on the far western frontier of the United States.

THE FRENCH AND INDIAN WAR

As colonists moved ever westward, settling on Native American hunting grounds, they did not pay much attention to the Native Americans' growing anger, or to the growing French military presence in the Ohio country beyond the mountains. A February 1754 message from the governor of Virginia alerted the North Carolina government to the threat of danger from the west.

Governor Robert Dinwiddie of Virginia had sent the young militia officer George Washington to the Ohio country to warn the French that they were trespassing on British territory. Washington returned home with the alarming information that the French refused to leave. On receiving Governor Dinwiddie's warning, the North Carolina legislature voted to spend money on western defense of their own colony and to send several hundred militiamen to help George Washington drive the French from the Ohio country.

The first battle in Pennsylvania in 1754 marked the beginning of a long world war whose battles raged on both sides of the Atlantic Ocean. France and Great Britain fought for control of territories in North America, the West Indies, Europe, and India. In America, the war came to be called the French and Indian War. In Europe the war was called the Seven Years' War. During the war, North Carolina militiamen served in campaigns from Virginia to New York.

The crushing defeat suffered by British and colonial troops under General Edward Braddock on July 9, 1755, left the western frontier under the control of the French and their Native American allies. North Carolina frontier dwellers endured attacks by Shawnee, Delaware, and other Native Americans from outside the colony. As their neighbors were killed or captured, hundreds of settlers abandoned their farms and fled to the east. Some took refuge behind the stockade of the Moravian town of Bethabara. The North

North Carolina militia built a log fort, Fort Dobbs, on Fourth Creek in an effort to protect the frontier from Native American attacks during the French and Indian War.

The Three Cherokees came over from the head of the River Savanna to London 1762.
Their Interpreter that was Poisoned

In 1762, three Cherokee chiefs traveled to London to seal their friendship with the British.

Carolina government ordered forts to be built along the frontier and recruited troops to man the forts. In 1758, the Cherokees joined the French side and began raiding frontier colonists. British troops came to the Carolina frontier and fought a series of skirmishes with the Cherokees.

Defeated in 1761, the Cherokees signed a treaty that gave them the land west of a line along the crest of the western mountains. Soon after the treaty was signed, white settlers began moving in on them. Within 50 years, about 3,000 Cherokees had been pushed into the far southwest corner of North Carolina. By the time the Revolution began, only about 500 Native Americans still lived east of the mountains, most on reservations. Many tribes had only a few dozen survivors after years of warfare and epidemics.

6.
REGULATORS AND REVOLUTIONARIES

The British finally defeated the French at Quebec in 1759 and later took control of Canada. In 1763 France and Great Britain signed a peace treaty giving the British control of much of North America east of the Mississippi River. The costly war with France had convinced the British government that the colonies should help pay the costs of sending soldiers to America to defend colonists against Native Americans. **Parliament** imposed taxes on the colonists, and this enraged them. People throughout the colonies believed that a distant Parliament had no right to tax them and was violating their right to self-government.

The first major new tax law was the Sugar **Act** of 1764. The act called for import and export duties, or taxes, to be paid on many trade goods, such as sugar, coffee, indigo, and animal hides. Next, in 1765 Parliament passed the Stamp Act. Under the Stamp Act, colonists had to pay to have most documents stamped, or risk arrest. Even newspapers had to have stamps. The Stamp Act affected colonists of all social classes.

Hundreds of North Carolinians demonstrated against the Stamp Act. Groups calling themselves the Sons of Liberty formed in North Carolina and throughout the colonies to organize protests and sabotage any efforts to enforce the Stamp Act. The North Carolina Sons of Liberty forced the colony's stamp agent to resign, and they prevented a ship from delivering stamps to the colony.

(November 20.) THE (Numb. 58.)

NORTH-CAROLINA GAZETTE.

WILMINGTON, November 20.

ON Saturday the 19th of laſt Month, about Seven of the Clock in the Evening, near Five Hundred People aſſembled together in this Town, and exhibited the Effigy of a certain HONOURABLE GENTLEMAN; and after letting it hang by the Neck for ſome Time, near the Court-Houſe, they made a large Bonfire with a Number of Tar-Barrels, &c. and committed it to the Flames.——The Reaſon aſſigned for the People's Diſlike to that Gentleman, was, from being informed of his having ſeveral Times expreſſed himſelf much in Favour of the STAMP-DUTY.——After the Effigy was conſumed, they went to every Houſe in Town, and bro't all the Gentlemen to the Bonfire, and inſiſted upon their drinking, LIBERTY, PROPERTY, AND NO STAMP-DUTY, and Confuſion to Lord B-te and all his Adherents, giving three Huzzas at the Concluſion of each Toaſt.——They continued together until 12 of the Clock, and then diſperſed, without doing any Miſchief. And,

On Thurſday, 31ſt of the ſame Month, in the Evening, a great Number of People again aſſembled, and produced an Effigy of LIBERTY, which they put into a Coffin, and marched in ſolemn Proceſſion with it to the Church-Yard, a Drum in Mourning beating before them; and the Town Bell, muffled, ringing a doleful Knell at the ſame Time;——But before they committed the Body to the Ground, they thought it adviſeable to feel its Pulſe; and when finding ſome Remains of Life, they returned back to a Bonfire ready prepared, placed the Effigy before it in a large Two-arm'd Chair, and concluded the Evening with great Rejoicings, on finding that LIBERTY had ſtill an Exiſtence in the COLONIES.——Not the leaſt Injury was offered to any Perſon.

On Saturday the 16th of this Inſt. WILLIAM HOUSTON, Eſq; Diſtributor of STAMPS for this Province, came to this Town; upon which three or four Hundred People immediately gathered together, with Drums beating and Colours flying, and repaired to the Houſe the ſaid STAMP-OFFICER put up at, and inſiſted upon knowing, "Whether he intended to execute his ſaid Office, or not?" He told them, "He ſhould be very ſorry to execute any Office diſagreeable to the People of the Province." But they, not content with ſuch a Declaration, carried him into the Court-Houſe, where he ſigned a Reſignation ſatisfactory to the Whole.

As ſoon as the STAMP-OFFICER had comply'd with their Deſire, they placed him in an Arm-Chair, carried him firſt round the Court-Houſe, giving three Huzzas at every Corner, and then proceeded with him round one of the Squares of the Town, and ſat him down at the Door of his Lodgings, formed themſelves in a large Circle round him, and gave him three Cheers: They then eſcorted him into the Houſe, where was prepared the beſt Liquors to be had, and treated him very genteely. In the Evening a large Bonfire was made, and no Perſon appeared in the Streets without having LIBERTY, in large Capital Letters, in his Hat.—— They had a large Table near the Bonfire, well furniſh'd with ſeveral Sorts of Liquors, where they drank in great Form, all the favourite AMERICAN Toaſts, giving three Cheers at the Concluſion of each. The whole was conducted with great Decorum, and not the leaſt Inſult offered to any Perſon.

B ¶ Immediately

——*Its Breed's the Title Page,*
That ſpeaks the Nature of a TRAGIC Volume !
_____ Shakeſ.

This is the Place to affix the STAMP.

North Carolina did not have a printing press until one began operating in New Bern in 1749. Until then, government documents were copied out by hand or printed in Williamsburg, Virginia. The weekly newspaper, the *North Carolina Gazette*, began publication in 1751. This article describes a protest against the Stamp Act.

When a British officer captured several merchant ships that lacked the proper stamped documents and held them in port near Wilmington, a band of armed men boarded the British vessel and forced the captain to release the ships.

Although the widespread protests caused Parliament to repeal the Stamp Act, Britain passed new tax laws. The British government insisted that Parliament had the right to impose taxes on the colonies. Since the colonists did not have elected officials to represent them in Parliament, they objected to what they called taxation without representation.

THE REGULATORS

While the colonists of eastern North Carolina resisted British authority, the mountain people in the western part of the colony objected to the authority of the colonial government. They could not afford the taxes, fees, and public work days imposed on them by comparatively wealthy public officials. In 1766, North Carolina's assembly had 61 representatives from the eastern counties of the prosperous Tidewater and Piedmont regions. The back-country mountain counties, which held about half the colony's population, were allowed to elect only 17 representatives. So they, too, felt they suffered under taxation without representation, not only by Britain, but also by North Carolina.

Aside from their few elected assemblymen, all other local officials—such as sheriffs, judges, militia officers, and clerks—were appointed by the colonial government.

Some frontier settlers tried to avoid paying taxes by running off the tax collector.

Local citizens in the western counties complained that their public officials were corrupt. They felt the officials too quickly confiscated citizens' farms when they were late paying taxes, without giving the farmers a chance to raise the money. In addition to making public complaints, angry citizens attacked and beat public officials on several occasions.

The colonial government made matters much worse, however, in 1767, by imposing new taxes to pay for construction of a governor's mansion. The two taxes, a poll tax on voters and a liquor tax, enraged western citizens and drove them to organize an association for "regulating public ... abuses of power." So they became known as the "Regulators." The Regulators demanded to meet with several sheriffs and inspect their books, to see if they were collecting too much money or keeping it for their personal use.

Governor William Tryon issued a warning to public officials to correct their behavior. He marched with the colonial militia to keep order at a series of controversial trials at Hillsborough (in present-day Orange County, east of Greensboro) in 1768. A New York lawyer and public

Tryon Palace, a mansion built for the governor with 15,000 pounds of taxpayers' money, especially angered the poor backcountry colonists and led to the formation of the Regulators. Tryon did not live in the mansion for long. He received a new job as royal governor of New York. The hated Edmund Fanning also moved to New York, as Tryon's secretary.

official, Edmund Fanning, stood accused of charging excessive fees, and a Quaker leader of the Regulators, Hermon Husband, was charged with "inciting the populace to rebellion." Possibly as many as 3,000 Regulators camped near the militia camp during the trials, but a violent confrontation was avoided because the court found Fanning guilty and Husband not guilty. Fanning was ordered to pay a small fine and resigned from his public position. The following year, western citizens elected several Regulators as assemblymen, including Hermon Husband.

In 1770, unrest again erupted at the courthouse in Hillsborough, where a number of cases involving Regulators were scheduled. A group of Regulators disrupted the courtroom, beat up Edmund Fanning, and destroyed his house. They attacked several other attorneys and ran Judge Richard Henderson out of town. The rioters then held mock trials and wrote insulting

Confrontation between Governor Tryon and the Regulators

comments in the court records. In New Bern, the assembly reacted by expelling Hermon Husband and passing a law aimed at preventing the Regulators from meeting. The Regulators then issued a series of threats against public officials and a death sentence against Fanning, stating that he should be killed on sight.

Governor Tryon again went on the march, leading about 1,000 colonial militiamen westward in 1771. About 2,000 Regulators had gathered near Alamance Creek, outside of present-day Greensboro. After giving the Regulators a last chance to withdraw, Tryon gave the order to fire. The militia, though outnumbered, was better trained and organized, and many Regulators fled under fire. The remaining Regulators were soundly defeated. Six of their leaders were tried and executed for treason. The Regulator movement broke up, with some accepting a government pardon and others moving farther west into Tennessee, out of the reach of the colonial government.

FROM BOYCOTT TO BATTLEFIELD

When not dealing with the rebellious Regulators, Governor Tryon faced a rebellious assembly. Objecting to British tax laws, the assembly considered joining the other colonies in a **boycott** of British goods. In an effort to prevent it, Tryon dissolved the assembly in 1769, but they met anyway and voted to participate in the boycott. Members of the Wilmington Sons of Liberty formed a committee to enforce the boycott. North Carolina also formed a Committee of Correspondence to share information with similar committees in the other colonies. The departure of Tryon to his new position as royal governor of New York had little effect on the rebellious assembly in North Carolina. The assembly refused to cooperate with the new governor, Josiah Martin.

Few colonists really wanted independence from Great Britain, as long as they could make their own laws and set their own taxes. Then in 1773 Parliament passed a law that gave one British tea seller, the struggling East India Company, special treatment. The East India Company was given a monopoly in the colonies, so that it could sell its tea more cheaply than any other dealer. The Committees of Correspondence went to work, spreading word of the

Opposite: This mocking cartoon portraying the so-called Edenton tea party was published in London in 1775. In October 1774, 51 women from five counties met in Edenton to sign a resolution supporting the actions of the provincial congress.

> BOYCOTT: AGREEMENT TO REFUSE TO BUY FROM OR SELL TO CERTAIN BUSINESSES

new law and the coming East India Company tea shipments. The Sons of Liberty throughout the colonies organized actions against the shipments.

The first such action, the famous Boston Tea Party, occurred in December 1773 with the dumping of a large tea shipment into Boston Harbor. When Britain responded to the Boston Tea Party by closing the port of Boston and placing Massachusetts under military rule, North Carolina sent a shipload of supplies to Boston's neighboring port, Salem. Many in the colonies began to argue that they would have to fight for independence from Great Britain. They planned a meeting of the colonies in Philadelphia, to take place in September 1774. This meeting became known as the First Continental Congress.

Governor Martin refused to let the assembly meet to choose delegates for the First Continental Congress, so the citizens of Wilmington held a mass meeting to set up their own "provincial congress." Despite Martin's efforts to forbid illegal meetings, counties throughout the colony elected a total of 71 delegates to the new provincial congress. Many of the new delegates had been members of the colonial assembly. The first provincial congress of North Carolina met on August 24, 1774, in New Bern, defiantly close to the governor's house. The delegates voted to boycott British goods and set up committees of safety to defend colonists' rights, and elected three delegates to attend the Congress in Philadelphia. The provincial congress also declared loyalty to King George III, saying that they were objecting only to the actions of Parliament.

Governor Martin called the old colonial assembly into session for what proved to be its last time in April 1775. When the assembly members, most of whom also served in the rebel provincial congress, refused to vote as he wished, Martin dissolved the assembly for good. A few weeks later, word arrived that the first shots of the American Revolution had been fired at Lexington, Massachusetts, on April 19, 1775. In New Bern, patriots entered the grounds of the governor's palace and hauled off several cannons. The governor had already sent his family to New York, and sensing that he had lost control of the colony, took refuge on a British ship.

From his ship, Martin called for colonists loyal to Britain to form an army and march to the coast to join

The site of the Moore's Creek bridge. The rebels removed planks to make it difficult for the loyalist forces to cross the creek. Many Scottish Highlanders joined the loyalist troops because they had to swear loyalty to Great Britain as a condition of their receiving land in North Carolina.

LOYALISTS: COLONISTS WHO WANTED AMERICA TO REMAIN A COLONY OF GREAT BRITAIN

with a British force. The patriots found out about the plan and assembled their own militia and Continental forces to stop them. The two forces confronted one another at Moore's Creek on February 27, 1776, and the patriots won an overwhelming victory over a force of about 1,600 **loyalists**. As a result, the British army stayed out of North Carolina for the first few years of the Revolution.

Three North Carolina delegates signed the Declaration of Independence at Philadelphia in July 1776. North Carolina adopted a constitution as an independent state in December 1776. The first state governor was Richard Caswell. At its first meeting in New Bern, the state government set about recruiting soldiers for the militia and the Continental Army. North Carolina contributed about 17,000 troops to the patriot cause.

In 1781, an important battle of the Revolution took place on North Carolina soil. At Guilford Court House, American General Nathanael Greene and his army had to retreat, but they had fought so hard and so damaged the British force commanded by Lord Cornwallis that it never won another victory.

The battle of Guilford Courthouse, March 15, 1781

EPILOGUE

North Carolina became the twelfth state to approve the United States Constitution on November 21, 1789. Three years later, the town of Raleigh was founded with the intention of making it the state capital.

Modern North Carolina has a population of about 7.5 million. About one-quarter of the population is black. North Carolina also has about 65,000 Native American residents, the highest Native American population among the eastern states. Most of North Carolina's remaining Cherokee Native Americans were forced to leave the state in 1830. About 8,000 Cherokees live on a reservation in the state's western mountains. A small group of Lumbee Native Americans, believed to be descendants of the lost colonists of Roanoke, lives near Pembroke.

About half of North Carolina's people live in rural areas and small towns. The other half live in major cities, including the capital, Raleigh, and Charlotte, Durham, Greensboro, Wilmington, and Winston-Salem. The cities of Wilmington and Morehead City have deepwater ports. The land of North Carolina was once covered in forests, but now only about half the land is wooded.

About a third of North Carolina's workers are employed in manufacturing such products as textiles, tobacco goods,

North Carolina tobacco field

furniture, chemicals, and electronic equipment. A major army base, Fort Bragg, is located near Fayetteville, and the important Marine Corps base, Camp Lejeune, is near Jacksonville. Several universities, including Duke University and the University of North Carolina, and industrial research and development centers, are clustered around Raleigh.

About three percent of the labor force works in agriculture. Tobacco is the main crop. North Carolina grows about 40% of the nation's tobacco. North Carolina's farms also raise corn, cotton, apples, hogs, and turkeys.

Both the seacoast and the Blue Ridge and Great Smoky Mountains attract numerous visitors from out of state. Visitors have many opportunities to learn about North Carolina's history. The Fort Raleigh National Historic Site on Roanoke Island, site of the Lost Colony, offers a reconstruction of part of the fort occupied by the colonists. Historic Bethabara, a reconstruction of the 1753 Moravian settlement, and Old Salem, a restored and reconstructed colonial village of 1766, are located at Winston-Salem. Town Creek Native American Mound, near Mount Gilead, offers a reconstructed Creek Native American site that was abandoned before the first colonists arrived. Guilford Court House National Military Park, at Greensboro, and Moore's Creek National Battlefield, near Wilmington, preserve the sites of North Carolina's Revolutionary War battles.

A Native american burial mound in Cherokee County, North Carolina. Historians believe that ancient Native americans built mounds as sites for ceremonial temples, chiefs' houses, and burials.

DATELINE

1524: Giovanni da Verrazano sights the North Carolina coast.

1540: Hernando De Soto's expedition passes through the mountains of North Carolina.

1584: The first English explorers, part of an expedition sponsored by Walter Raleigh, set foot on the coast of present-day North Carolina. It is included in a vast area that Raleigh calls Virginia.

1585: A second expedition sails to "Virginia." A colonial outpost of 108 men is established on Roanoke Island.

1586: After a hungry winter, most of the men leave Roanoke with Sir Francis Drake. Only days later, an English supply ship arrives and leaves 15 men on Roanoke.

1587: Sir Walter Raleigh sends a group of 117 men, women, and children, led by John White, to colonize Virginia. Against their wishes, the colonists are left on Roanoke Island. They find the island deserted. White returns to England to seek help.

1590: John White overcomes numerous obstacles to return to Roanoke. The colonists are gone, having left a one-word message.

1607: A group of English settlers establish the first permanent English colony at Jamestown, Virginia, and begin an unsuccessful search for the lost Roanoke colonists.

1629: King Charles I grants a huge territory, called Carolana, to Sir Robert Heath.

MARCH 24, 1663: King Charles II grants a charter to eight of his loyal supporters, renaming the territory Carolina.

1669: The Fundamental Constitutions of Carolina take effect, granting religious liberty to the colonists.

SEPTEMBER 22, 1711: Tuscarora Native Americans attack and kill settlers in an effort to drive them from the colony.

1712: Carolina is divided into two separate colonies, North Carolina and South Carolina. The Tuscarora Indians and the colonists sign a treaty, but members of the militia break the treaty by capturing Indians and selling them into slavery. The war resumes.

1713: The Tuscarora War ends after forces from South Carolina win a decisive victory.

1729: North Carolina becomes a royal colony.

1767: The Regulator movement arises in western North Carolina in protest against corrupt local officials accused of charging extra fees and pocketing public money.

1771: The Regulators disband after their defeat by Governor Tryon's militia at the Battle of Alamance.

FEBRUARY 27, 1776: Patriots soundly defeat loyalists at Moore's Creek.

DECEMBER 1776: North Carolina adopts a constitution and declares itself an independent state.

MARCH 15, 1781: The Battle of Guilford Courthouse results in an American defeat but severely weakens the British forces.

NOVEMBER 21, 1789: North Carolina becomes the twelfth state to accept the United States Constitution.

Glossary

ACT: law, so called because it is made by an act of government

ANGLICAN: belonging to the Church of England, a Protestant church and the state church of England

ASSEMBLY: lower house of a legislature, with delegates elected by the voters

BOYCOTT: agreement to refuse to buy from or sell to certain businesses

BRITISH: nationality of a person born in Great Britain; people born in England are called "English."

CHARTER: document containing the rules for running an organization

ELITE: chosen; a group of people considered to have high status because of their birth, wealth, education, or social class

EPIDEMIC: widespread outbreak of contagious disease; for example, in 1738, a smallpox epidemic killed half of all Cherokee Indians

FEUDAL: system in medieval Europe under which landless farmers lived and worked on land owned by lords

FREEMEN: white, taxpaying males of at least 21 years of age who possessed all the rights of citizenship, such as the right to vote, hold public office, or own land

FRONTIER: newest place of settlement, located the farthest away from the center of population

GREAT BRITAIN: nation formed by England, Wales, Scotland, and Northern Ireland; the term "Great Britain" came into use when England and Scotland formally unified in 1707.

INDIANS: name given to all Native Americans at the time Europeans first came to America, because it was believed that America was actually a close neighbor of India

LEGISLATURE: group of representatives elected to make laws

LOYALISTS: colonists who wanted America to remain a colony of Great Britain

MILITIA: group of citizens not normally part of the army who join together to defend their land in an emergency

NATIVE AMERICANS: people who had been living in America for thousands of years at the time the first Europeans arrived

NAVIGATION: science of figuring out one's position and direction when traveling on the ocean

NOBILITY: members of the high British social class just below royalty, possessing titles or ranks that were either inherited or given by the king or queen

PARLIAMENT: legislature of Great Britain

PIONEERS: first settlers in a new territory

PIRACY: attacking ships at sea, with the aim of stealing the vessels and their cargo

PLANTER: owner of a large estate, farmed by slaves, called a plantation

POUND: the currency, or form of money, used by the British

PRIVATEER: privately-owned ship with government permission to attack the ships of enemy nations during wartime

PROPRIETOR: private owner

PROTESTANT: member of any Christian church that has broken away from Roman Catholic or Eastern Orthodox control

QUAKER: originally a term of mockery given to members of the Society of Friends, a Christian group founded in England around 1650

SCOTCH-IRISH / SCOTTISH HIGHLANDERS: Scottish people who settled in northern Ireland during the early 1600s. Many were driven by poverty to emigrate to America. Scottish Highlanders were natives of the highlands of Scotland who emigrated to America, many after losing a rebellion in Scotland.

SUBSISTENCE: producing just enough food or income to survive

WEST INDIES: islands of the Caribbean Sea, so called because the first European visitors thought they were near India

FURTHER READING

Long, Cathryn J. *The Cherokee*. San Diego: Luconn.nt Books, 2000.

Quiri, Patricia R. *The Algonquians*. Danbury, CT: Franklin Watts, 1992.

Smith, Carter, ed. *Daily Life: A Source Book on Colonial America*. Brookfield, Conn.: Millbrook Press, 1991.

Smith, Carter, ed. *Explorers and Settlers: A Source Book on Colonial America*. Brookfield, Conn.: Millbrook Press, 1991.

Tunis, Edwin. *Colonial Living*. Baltimore: Johns Hopkins University Press, 1999.

WEBSITES

http://www.americaslibrary.gov
Select "Jump back in time" for links to history activities

http://library.thinkquest.org/J002559/
How Do You Lose a Colony?

http://www.ncgov.com
Visit the official website of North Carolina, with a Kid's Page

http://www.thinkquest.org/library/JR_index.html
Find links to numerous student-designed sites about American colonial history

BIBLIOGRAPHY

Fenn, Elizabeth A., and Peter H. Wood. *Natives & Newcomers: The Way We Lived in North Carolina before 1770*. Chapel Hill: University of North Carolina Press, 1983.

Gallay, Alan. *Voices of the Old South: Eyewitness Accounts, 1528–1861*. Athens: University of Georgia Press, 1994.

Jones, H.G. *North Carolina Illustrated, 1524–1984*. Chapel Hill: University of North Carolina Press, 1983.

Leffler, Hugh T. and William S. Powell. *Colonial North Carolina: A History*. New York: Charles Scribner's Sons, 1973.

Middleton, Richard. *Colonial America: A History, 1607–1760*. Cambridge, Mass.: Blackwell, 1992.

Miller, Lee. *Roanoke: Solving the Mystery of the Lost Colony*. New York: Arcade Publishing, 2000.

Salley, Alexander S., Jr. *Narratives of Early Carolina, 1650–1708*. New York: Charles Scribner's Sons, 1911.

Taylor, Alan. *American Colonies*. New York: Viking, 2001.

The American Heritage History of the Thirteen Colonies. New York: American Heritage Co., 1967.

INDEX